SNAKES

Vipers

by Linda George

Consultants:
The staff of Black Hills Reptile Gardens
Rapid City, South Dakota

**CAPSTONE
HIGH-INTEREST
BOOKS**

an imprint of Capstone Press
Mankato, Minnesota

Capstone High-Interest Books are published by Capstone Press
151 Good Counsel Drive, P.O. Box 669, Mankato, Minnesota 56002
http://www.capstone-press.com

Library of Congress Cataloging-in-Publication Data
George, Linda.
    Vipers/by Linda George.
    p. cm.—(Snakes)
    Includes bibliographical references and index (p.48).
    ISBN 0-7368-0910-4
    1. Viperidae—Juvenile literature. [1. Poisonous snakes. 2. Snakes.]
I. Title. II. Animals and the environment. Snakes.
QL666.O69 G468 2002
597.96'3—dc21   2001000048

Summary: Describes the physical attributes, habitat, and hunting and mating methods of vipers.

Editorial Credits
Blake Hoena, editor; Lois Wallentine. product planning editor; Timothy Halldin, cover designer and illustrator; Katy Kudela, photo researcher

Photo Credits
Allen Blake Sheldon, 6, 10, 12, 35, 39
Cheryl A. Ertelt, 27, 40
Frederick D. Atwood, 24
Jim Merli/Visuals Unlimited, 32
Joe McDonald/TOM STACK & ASSOCIATES, cover, 9, 18–19, 20, 28
Joe McDonald/Visuals Unlimited, 15, 31, 36, 44
Ken Lucas/Visuals Unlimited, 23
Michael Cardwell/Extreme Wildlife Photography, 16

2 3 4 5 6 07 06 05 04 03 02

Table of Contents

Yellow areas represent the range of snakes within the Viperinae subfamily.

Fast Facts about Vipers

Scientific Name: Vipers are members of the Viperidae family. This scientific group is divided into three subfamilies. "True" vipers belong to the Viperinae subfamily.

Size: Vipers average between 3 and 5 feet (.9 and 1.5 meters) long. But some vipers may be as small as 1 foot (.3 meter). Other vipers may grow to be more than 7 feet (2.1 meters).

Range:	"True" vipers live in Europe, Asia, and Africa.
Description:	Vipers have hollow fangs. These long teeth are hinged. They lie flat against the roof of a viper's mouth when its mouth is closed. The fangs swing forward and lock into place when the viper is ready to bite.
Habitat:	Vipers mostly live in dry areas such as deserts, savannas, and mountains. But some vipers live in swampy areas and rain forests.
Food:	Vipers eat rodents such as mice and rats. They also may eat other small animals such as birds, frogs, and lizards.
Habits:	Vipers ambush their prey. They lie in wait for prey to pass by before they strike.
Reproduction:	A group of newborn snakes is called a clutch. Between six and 60 vipers are born in a clutch. Most vipers are ovoviviparous. Their eggs develop and hatch inside the female's body. Females then give live birth to their young. A few vipers are oviparous. They lay eggs that develop and hatch outside the female's body.

CHAPTER 1

Vipers

Vipers are venomous. They inject venom into animals they bite. Venom kills prey. It also can seriously harm or kill animals that threaten vipers.

Snake Families

All snakes are reptiles. Alligators, crocodiles, lizards, and turtles also are reptiles.

More than 2,300 snake species exist in the world. A species is a specific animal or plant.

Scientists divide snake species with similar features into families. Vipers are members of the Viperidae family. More than 200 snake species are in this group.

Vipers are members of the Viperidae family.

The Viperidae family includes vipers and pit vipers. Snakes in this family have long, hollow fangs. Venom flows through the fangs and into the snake's prey.

Snakes in the Viperidae family also have fangs that are hinged. The fangs lie flat against the roof of a snake's mouth when its mouth is closed. The fangs swing forward and lock into place when the snake is ready to bite.

Viperidae Subfamilies

Scientists divide the Viperidae family into three subfamilies. Snakes in these groups are closely related. But important differences separate them.

Snakes in the Craotalinae subfamily are called pit vipers. This group includes Asian pit vipers, bushmasters, rattlesnakes, and cottonmouths. Pit vipers have heat-sensing facial pits. These holes are between the snakes' eyes and nostrils. They allow pit vipers to sense

Rattlesnakes have heat-sensing facial pits.

Vipers such as the saw-scaled viper do not have heat-sensing facial pits.

the warmth given off by an animal's body. Pit vipers use this ability to locate prey.

Azemiopinae is the second subfamily. The Fea's viper is the only member of this group. The Fea's viper does not have heat-sensing pits. But it has some features that are similar to pit vipers. These features include large head scales.

Viperinae is the third subfamily. Snakes in this group are called "true" vipers. These snakes do not have heat-sensing pits like pit vipers. Snakes in the Viperinae subfamily include saw-scaled vipers, common adders, gaboon vipers, and puff adders. This book discusses vipers in the Viperinae subfamily.

Viper Genera

Scientists further divide snake families and subfamilies into genera. More than 60 snake species are in the Viperinae subfamily. These snakes are divided into 10 genera.

Vipera is the largest genus in the Viperinae subfamily. About 20 snake species are members of this group. Some snakes in the *Vipera* genus are known for living farther north than any other snake species. The European adder can even be found north of the Arctic Circle.

CHAPTER 2

Viper Species

Vipers have stocky bodies and short tails. They vary greatly in color and length. Vipers have wide, triangle-shaped heads. Their heads have this shape because of their venom glands. These organs produce venom. They are located toward the back and sides of a viper's head.

Saw-Scaled Viper

Echis carinatus is the scientific name for the saw-scaled viper. This snake gets its name from the sound its rough scales make. When threatened, the saw-scaled snake forms a figure eight with its body. The snake's scales then rub against each other. This action makes

The saw-scaled viper's rough scales make a hissing sound when rubbed against each other.

a loud hissing noise. The sound warns other animals that the saw-scaled viper may strike.

Saw-scaled vipers are brown, beige, or gray. They have a dark brown or red-brown zigzag pattern on their back. Saw-scaled vipers are between 2 and 2.5 feet (.6 and .8 meter) long.

Desert-Horned Viper

The scientific name for the desert-horned viper is *Cerastes cerastes*. This snake is called horned because it usually has a horn-shaped scale above each eye.

Desert-horned vipers are yellow-brown or light gray. Their coloring matches the color of the sand where they live. Desert-horned snakes grow to be about 2 feet (.6 meter) long.

Russell's Viper

The scientific name for the Russell's viper is *Vipera russellii*. This snake is named after Dr. Patrick Russell. In 1790, he discovered the Russell's viper in Asia.

The Russell's viper has deadly venom. It is a member of India's "Big Four." This group also includes the cobra, the krait, and the saw-scaled

The Russell's viper is one of the most venomous snakes in the world.

viper. These snakes are considered the four most venomous snakes in India. Russell's vipers and cobras cause more snake bite deaths per year than all other snakes in the world combined.

Russell's vipers usually are brown-yellow or gray. They have dark brown spots on their sides and back. These spots have a black and white outer edge.

Puff adders swell their bodies with air when threatened.

Gaboon Viper

Bitis gabonica is the scientific name for the gaboon viper. This snake is one of the largest vipers. It may grow to be 7 feet (2.1 meters) long. The gaboon viper also has longer fangs than any other snake. Its fangs may grow to be 2 inches (5 centimeters) long.

Gaboon vipers have unusual coloring. They often are a shade of light brown. They have spots along their back and sides. These spots may be shaped like diamonds, rectangles, or triangles. The spots are black or a shade of brown, green, red, or purple.

Common Adder

The scientific name for the common adder is *Vipera berus*. This snake also is known as the European adder. It lives in many parts of Europe.

Common adders are gray, olive, or brown. They have a dark brown zigzag pattern on their back. Common adders usually are less than 2 feet (.6 meter) long.

Puff Adder

The scientific name for the puff adder is *Bitis arientans*. People call this snake the puff adder because it breathes in air when threatened. This action makes the snake's body swell in size. The puff adder then makes a loud hissing sound as it lets out the air.

Puff adders are a mixture of brown and black. They have light and dark lines along the width of their body. Puff adders usually are between 3 and 4 feet (.9 and 1.2 meters) long.

Gaboon Viper

Tail

Head

CHAPTER 3

Habitat

People sometimes call snakes in the Viperinae subfamily "Old World" vipers. These snakes live in most parts of Asia, Africa, and Europe. But they do not live in North or South America.

Adders

Common adders have a wide range. Like all adders, they live mostly in dry areas. Common adders live in both Europe and Asia. They are the only venomous snake that lives in Great Britain and northern Europe. They also are the only snake that lives north of the Arctic Circle.

Puff adders live mostly in sub-Saharan Africa.

Puff adders live throughout sub-Saharan Africa. These dry areas are near and around the Sahara Desert.

Vipers

Russell's vipers live in the Asian countries of India, China, Pakistan, and Bangladesh. They also live in Thailand, Malaysia, Vietnam, Myanmar, and Taiwan. Russell's vipers often hide in brush, termite mounds, rocky areas, or rodent burrows. Animals such as mice and rats live in these holes in the ground. Russell's vipers often are found along the edges of fields where they hunt rodents.

Saw-scaled vipers live in the Middle East and eastern Africa. They also live in northern India and Pakistan. Saw-scaled vipers mostly live in dry areas such as savannas. They also live in woodlands and plains. Saw-scaled vipers seem to prefer areas with sandy and rocky soil. They bury themselves in the sand to hide.

Desert-horned vipers live mostly in the Middle East and northern Africa. They seem to prefer dry, sandy areas. Like saw-scaled

Desert-horned vipers often bury themselves to hide.

vipers, desert-horned vipers bury themselves in the sand to hide.

Gaboon vipers live mostly in central and southern Africa. They live in rain forests and wooded areas. Gaboon vipers often hide in fallen leaves on the forest floor.

CHAPTER 4

Hunting

Most vipers are nocturnal. They are active and hunt at night. The animals they hunt also are most active at night.

During the day, vipers often rest to avoid the sun's heat and to hide from predators. Predators hunt other animals for food. Vipers may rest in rodent burrows, old termite mounds, rocky areas, piles of leaves, or under rotting logs.

Vipers' Prey

Vipers eat a variety of prey. They often eat lizards or rodents. But vipers also eat birds, frogs, and insects.

Vipers lie in wait to ambush prey.

A snake's size often determines its prey. Some of the smaller vipers may eat large insects, scorpions, and spiders. Gaboon vipers are one of the largest vipers. They often eat lizards and rodents.

Ambushing Prey

Vipers have thick bodies. This shape makes them slower than many other snakes. Because of their slow speed, they do not actively hunt prey. Instead, they ambush their prey. Vipers lie in wait for prey to pass by before they strike.

Camouflage helps vipers hide from prey. Their coloring blends in with their natural surroundings. Gaboon vipers' coloring helps them blend in with leaves on the forest floor. Desert-horned and saw-scaled vipers are similar in color to the sand in their surroundings. These snakes bury themselves in sand or loose soil as they wait for prey.

Senses for Hunting

Vipers do not see as well as people do. But they can detect light, shapes, colors, and movement. This ability helps them find prey.

Vipers use their tongue to help them smell.

Vipers also cannot hear sounds as people do. Instead, vipers feel vibrations in the ground and air. These sensations help them know when prey is near.

The Jacobson's organ is located on the roof of a snake's mouth. A snake uses this organ to smell. A viper flicks out its tongue to collect scent particles in the air or on the ground. The tongue carries the scents to the Jacobson's

Vipers inject venom into their prey.

organ. The Jacobson's organ then determines what the scent particles are from. A viper can smell prey with its Jacobson's organ. A male viper can smell females that are ready to mate.

Biting Prey

A viper strikes when prey passes by. The viper injects venom into its prey as it bites. Venom flows through its long, hollow fangs and into the wound created by its bite.

Vipers inject venom into their prey to kill the animal. After biting, some vipers let go of their prey. The animal then may try to escape. But vipers do not chase after their prey. Instead, they follow the animal's scent to find it after it dies.

Other vipers hold onto prey after biting. These vipers then are able to inject more venom into their prey if needed.

Venom

Vipers control the amount of venom that they inject into prey. This amount often depends on the size of their prey. They inject more venom into larger prey.

The venom then spreads through a victim's body. It travels through the bloodstream. Venom also spreads through cell tissue.

Viper venom mainly is hemotoxic. It affects the circulatory system. This system includes the blood, blood vessels, and the heart. The venom destroys blood cells and blood vessels. Bite victims then start to bleed internally. This action causes the heart to beat rapidly and weaken. Prey may die from heart failure or blood loss.

Viper venom also may affect other parts of the body. It can destroy nerve tissue and the body's cell tissue. Each viper's venom has a different effect on its victims. Many vipers also have venom that specifically affects the animals that they hunt as food.

Eating Prey

Vipers do not chew their food. Like all snakes, they swallow prey whole. They often swallow prey head first. Their prey's limbs then fold neatly against the body. This positioning makes it easier for vipers to swallow prey.

A viper can swallow prey that is larger than its mouth. Ligaments connect its upper and lower jaws. These stretchy bands of tissue allow a viper's jaws to separate as it swallows prey. Strong throat muscles then pull the viper's prey into its stomach.

Vipers can eat prey that is larger than the size of their mouth.

Acids within a viper's stomach digest its prey. These chemicals break down food to be used by the body. Vipers often rest after eating to allow their food to digest.

CHAPTER 5

Mating

Snakes are cold-blooded. Their body temperature is similar to that of their surroundings.

Vipers that live in cold climates need to hibernate to survive. They burrow underground and remain inactive during the winter. Hibernation allows vipers to survive cold weather and lack of food.

Vipers wake from hibernation in the spring. They then seek a mate. Females give off a scent that allows males to find them. This scent often attracts more then one male. The males then take part in a combat dance.

Some vipers give live birth to their young.

Combat Dance

Male vipers often take part in a combat dance during mating season. This action determines which male mates with a female viper.

The dance starts when one male viper tries to crawl past or over another male viper. The snakes then wrap around each other. They raise their heads and the front halves of their bodies high into the air. They do not bite each other during this dance. Instead, they try to climb on top of each other. Eventually, one snake succeeds and holds down the other one. The losing snake then leaves.

Eggs

A viper's habitat determines whether it lays eggs or not. Most vipers that live in warm climates are oviparous. These vipers lay eggs that develop and hatch outside their body.

Vipers that live in cold climates often are ovoviviparous. Their eggs develop and hatch inside the female's body. This action keeps the eggs warm. Eggs need warmth to survive and develop.

Some vipers are both ovoviviparous and oviparous. These snakes include the levant viper.

The levant viper is both ovoviviparous and oviparous.

Young

Most vipers' young hatch or are born in late summer. Six to 60 vipers may be born in a clutch. Young vipers range in size from 5 to 10 inches (13 to 25 centimeters) long.

Young vipers care for themselves after they are born. They find their own prey and shelter. They often eat insects and small animals.

CHAPTER 6

Vipers and People

A viper's camouflage keeps it well hidden. People often approach a viper or step on it before they see the snake.

Many vipers bite when threatened or approached. Vipers such as the puff adder and saw-scaled viper readily bite. But other vipers such as the gaboon viper do not bite as often. The gaboon viper relies on camouflage and its size for protection. This snake only bites as a last resort.

Viper Bites

Viper bites can be dangerous to people. More than 80 percent of the people bitten

The saw-scaled viper has deadly venom.

by saw-scaled vipers die. Puff adders are one of the leading causes of snake bites in Africa. Russell's vipers also have venom that is deadly to people.

Viper bites usually produce sharp, burning pain at the site of the bite. This area then starts to swell. The swelling spreads toward the heart as the venom travels through the body. The area around the bite may become blue, green, purple, or black. These bruises are caused by bleeding under the skin.

The biggest danger from a viper bite is the weakening effect it has on the victim's heart. Loss of blood from internal bleeding also is a danger. People who have been severely poisoned may bleed from the eyes, nose, ears, and mouth. They may die from loss of blood.

Benefits of Vipers

Vipers may be harmful to people. But vipers also provide some benefits.

Many vipers eat rodents such as rats and mice. These animals may spread diseases. They also may eat farmers' crops. Vipers help keep rodent populations down.

Scientists take venom from snakes to create antivenin.

Scientists also make antivenin from viper venom. Doctors use these medicines to treat snake bites.

Myths

Many myths are told about vipers. One of these false stories says that young vipers crawl into their mother's stomach when threatened. This story is not true. The acids in their mother's

Puff adders readily bite when threatened.

stomach would digest the young vipers as though they were food.

In some Asian countries, people believe that viper flesh is a cure for diseases such as neuralgia and tuberculosis. Neuralgia is nerve pain. Tuberculosis is a lung disease. These people eat viper broth and boiled viper flesh. But these foods have not been proven to cure these diseases.

Viper Warnings

Vipers have few predators. Predatory birds and other snakes may eat vipers. Mongooses hunt vipers. These animals are known for their ability to kill venomous snakes. Monitors also eat vipers. These large lizards live mostly in Africa and southern Asia.

Vipers rely on camouflage to hide from danger. They also have several means of warning other animals that they might bite. The saw-scaled viper rubs its scales against each other. This action creates a hissing sound.

The gaboon viper does not bite as readily as most other vipers. But when threatened, it puffs up its body and hisses loudly. The puff adder also puffs up its body when threatened. This action makes the snake appear larger. Predators then may be less likely to attack the puff adder.

Vipers can be dangerous. Many are quick to bite. Many also have venom that is deadly to people. Vipers should never be handled by anyone who is not a snake expert.

Words to Know

acids (ASS-ids)—substances in an animal's stomach that help it break down food

ambush (AM-bush)—to hide and then attack; vipers ambush their prey.

camouflage (KAM-uh-flahzh)—coloring or covering that makes animals, people, and objects look like their surroundings

digest (dye-JEST)—to break down food so it can be used by the body

family (FAM-uh-lee)—a group of animals with similar features

genus (JEE-nuhss)—a group of closely related animals or plants

habitat (HAB-uh-tat)—the place and natural conditions in which plants and animals live

hibernate (HYE-bur-nate)—to be inactive during the winter; vipers often burrow into the ground to hibernate.

nocturnal (nok-TUR-nuhl)—active at night

oviparous (oh-VIP-uh-rus)—laying eggs that develop and hatch outside the female's body

ovoviviparous (oh-voh-vye-VIP-uh-rus)—having eggs that develop and hatch inside the female's body; ovoviviparous animals give live birth to their young.

predator (PRED-uh-tur)—an animal that hunts other animals for food

prey (PRAY)—an animal hunted by another animal for food

species (SPEE-sheez)—a specific type of animal or plant

venom (VEN-uhm)—poison produced by some snakes; venom passes into a victim's body when a venomous snake bites.

To Learn More

Ethan, Eric. *Vipers*. Fangs! Milwaukee: Gareth Stevens, 1995.

Mattison, Christopher. *Snake.* New York: DK Publishing, 1999.

McDonald, Mary Ann, and Joe McDonald. *Rattlesnakes*. Animals and the Environment. Mankato, Minn.: Capstone High-Interest Books, 1996.

Stone, Lynn M. *Snakes with Venom*. Eye to Eye with Snakes. Vero Beach, Fla.: Rourke, 2000.

Useful Addresses

Black Hills Reptile Gardens
P.O. Box 620
Rapid City, SD 57709

Milwaukee Public Museum
Herpetology Department
800 West Wells Street
Milwaukee, WI 53233-1478

Smithsonian National Zoological Park
3001 Connecticut Avenue NW
Washington, DC 20008

Toronto Zoo
361A Old Firch Avenue
Scarborough, ON M1B 5K7
Canada

Internet Sites

Black Hills Reptile Gardens
http://www.reptile-gardens.com

Enchanted Learning.com—Snake Printouts
http://www.enchantedlearning.com/subjects/
   reptiles/snakes/printouts.shtml

Toronto Zoo
http://www.torontozoo.com

Index